# NEVER MIND
## SKY THE BLUES

### *The Ultimate COVENTRY CITY*

## QUIZ BOOK

## MICHAEL KEANE

T0346845

First published 2016

The History Press
97 St George's Place, Cheltenham, Gloucestershire, GL5 2QG
www.thehistorypress.co.uk

British Library Cataloguing in Publication Data.
A catalogue record for this book is available from the British Library.

ISBN 978 0 7509 6020 5

Typesetting and origination by The History Press
Printed by TJ Books Limited, Padstow, Cornwall.

MIX
Paper | Supporting
responsible forestry
FSC® C013056
www.fsc.org

All images are the property of Michael Keane

# Contents

# **Round**

# **1**

# **Around the World**

Although the club has concentrated on academy players in recent cash-strapped years, City managers have often recruited from far and wide to bring the best overseas talent. See how many of these global stars left a lasting impression …

1   Which City striker from the mid-1990s, once nicknamed the 'new Pele', was the Golden Ball winner at the 1991 U17 World Cup in Italy?

2   Name the ex-Bosnian soldier who patrolled the Highfield Road defences from 1999–2004?

3   Which Icelandic ex-handball player did City boss Chris Coleman bring to the Ricoh Arena in the summer of 2008?

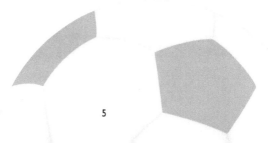

4 Two stars of the 1998 World Cup were brought to Highfield Road by Gordon Strachan twelve months later. Name them.

5 Which Romanian striker became the first Coventry City player to score at the World Cup finals in France in 1998? Do you know who he scored against?

6 After hitting 32 goals in his native country's top flight, which Peruvian striker was snapped up by City at the turn of the millennium?

7 Name the two City players who represented Trinidad and Tobago at the 2006 World Cup.

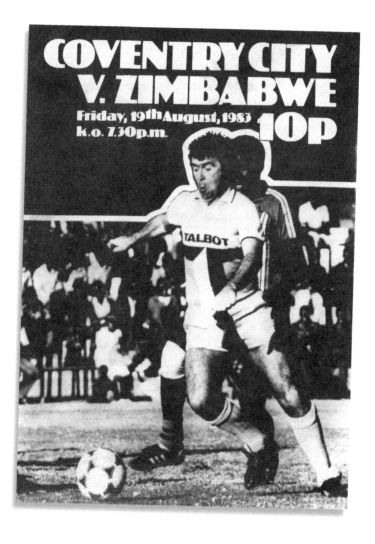

7

8   Name the Maltese-born City striker who was nicknamed the 'Mosquito', and once memorably put Manchester United to the sword?

9   Which Sky Blues Faroes Island international became the first player to score at the newly opened Ricoh Arena in August 2005?

10  Name the Zimbabwean striker spotted by John Sillett on a pre-season tour in the late 1980s, who went on to terrorise premiership defenders for nearly six years?

# Round

# 2

# **Banana Skins**

While the Sky Blues have now been away from the top flight of English football for a decade and a half, their scalp is still a sought-after one for lower-league opposition. Sadly, the days of slipping up on cup-tie banana skins seems to be showing no sign of stopping any time soon …

1  In November 1961, Third Division City hosted King's Lynn of the Southern League Premier Division in an FA Cup second-round match. Which guest watched the nightmarish 2–1 defeat to the part-timers from the back of the stand, and why was he there?

2  City's next non-league disaster came against Sutton United at Gander Green Lane in January 1989. What was the profession of Sutton's very well-read manager, Barrie Williams?

3    Unlike most managers, Williams liked to include lines
     penned by famous writers in his programme notes.
     Try and complete these famous Kipling lines that Williams
     presciently included in his programme notes that day:

     *It ain't the individual nor the Army as a whole,*
     *it's the everlasting _____ of every bloomin' soul*

4    Matthew Hanlan rocked City to their foundations with his
     winning goal at Gander Green Lane. He wasn't a butcher,
     a baker or a candlestick maker, but what was his job?

5    For what reason did City boss John Sillett declare that
     Sunday would be an even worse day for his players?

6    What position were City in the old First Division when
     they played their cup tie at Sutton?

7    Unfortunately, Steven Pressley's 2014 Sky Blues
     vintage were at it again, losing a first-round cup tie
     against Worcester City. Rookie keeper Lee Burge was
     playing in his first FA Cup tie, but how many senior
     appearances had he made, up to and including the
     Worcester debacle?

8 Why was Burge given a straight red card in the 39th minute?

9 How did City's man-mountain captain Réda Johnson fluff his lines just before the interval?

10 When City boss Steven Pressley next spoke to the press he pulled no punches in his withering assessment of some of his squad. Complete these Pressley lines:

*Certain players are in a _____ _____ and they'll be _____ _____ _____ football club.*

07727

F.A. CUP 3rd ROUND

**SUTTON UNITED**

v

**COVENTRY CITY**

at the Borough Sportsground, Gander Green Lane, Sutton
on Saturday 7 January 1989. K.O. 2.00 p.m.

Admission to Ground  **£5**

Sold subject to ground rules as display

# Odd One Out

The following groups of significant figures from Coventry's history are mostly connected to each other. The trick is to work out which is not keeping the right company, which one sticks out like a sore thumb …

1  Under Jimmy Hill in the 1960s, Coventry became known for the innovative ways they looked after their fans. Which of these Sky Blue ruses from the '60s is the odd one out?

> *Sky Blue pools*      *Sky Blue specials*
>
> *Sky Blue beer and chips*      *Sky Blue Rose*

2  Which three of these City stars have shared a proud moment?

> *John Sillett*      *Bobby Gould*
>
> *Dave Phillips*      *Gordon Strachan*

3  Which one of these City players is the odd one out and why?

   *Matthew Pennington*    *Phil Babb*

   *Kenny Sansom*    *David Burrows*

4  Which of these city stars did not quite accomplish what the others did?

   *Cyrille Regis*    *Danny Thomas*

   *Steve Froggatt*    *Dion Dublin*

5  Which one of these City keepers does not share a trait with the other three?

   *Michael Quirke*    *Chris Kirkland*

   *Lee Burge*    *Keiren Westwood*

6   Which of these non-league teams that City have faced over the years is the odd one out and why?

Woking                      Sutton United

King's Lynn                 Worcester City

7   How is one of these sponsors different to the others?

Subaru cars                 Talbot cars

Jaguar cars                 Peugeot cars

8   Which one of these distinguished City players did not quite cut the mustard with the other three?

Steve Staunton              Kevin Kilbane

Stern John                  Magnus Hedman

9   Which one of these difficulties did Steven Pressley not
    have to deal with during his tenure?

> A 10-point deduction          46 away games
>
> Transfer embargoes            A gypsy curse

10  Which one of these 2014–15 players stands apart and why?

> Ryan Allsop                Dominic Samuel
>
> Jim O'Brien                Sanmi Odelusi
>
> Matthew Pennington         Chris Stokes
>
> Gary Madine                Nick Proschwitz
>
> Grant Ward                 Mohamed Coulibaly

# Round 4

# **Glory Days**

Although following Coventry City in their top-flight days seemed like backing the perennial underdog, just like every dog, City did sometimes have their day. If you're old enough, enjoy some glorious memories that are about to come flooding back – if you're not old enough, there's always YouTube!

1 Name the two City strikers who bagged winning hat-tricks against Liverpool in the 1980s and 1990s.

2 After twenty-four unsuccessful visits, City secured their first ever win at Anfield in November 1989, who headed home the winner from whose left-wing cross?

3 In 1983, City hammered the soon-to-be European Champions Liverpool 4–0. Nine years later, in 1992, City went one better and thumped the Reds 5–1. Which City boss masterminded both maulings of the Anfield men?

First target

EUROPE

17

4  On a bright Sunday morning in 1985, which recently crowned league champions and cup winners were thrashed 4–1 by City? What was significant about it?

5  When the then Premier League champions, Blackburn Rovers, came to a snowbound Highfield Road in December 1995, how many times was the orange ball put into Tim Flowers' net?

6  Ian Wallace and Mick Ferguson were probably City's best striking partnership in the top-flight years until Dion Dublin and Darren Huckerby emerged twenty years later. In total, Wallace and Ferguson hit 40 goals in 1978; did Dublin and Huckerby score more or less between them in 1998?

7  When Darren Huckerby scored his dazzling winner against Man United at Christmas 1997, what did his goal make the score? What had the score been with 4 minutes remaining?

8 In December 1999, the Sky Blues famously beat reigning champions Arsenal 3–2 in a Christmas cracker at Highfield Road. Name the three star internationals who scored for City that day.

9 When City were relegated from the Premier League, in 2001, who was their leading top-flight scorer?

10 Name the three City players who were capped for England while playing in the top flight for Coventry.

# sky blue

## MATCHDAY MAGAZINE
SATURDAY 15TH DECEMBER 1979 — 3.00p.m.

Picture by
Bob Thomas

## MANCHESTER UTD 30p
OFFICIAL MATCHDAY MAGAZINE OF COVENTRY CITY F.C.

# Round 5

# **Narrow Escapes**

Ten times in total, City took brinkmanship to new heights as they avoided dropping through the relegation trapdoor on the last day of the season. Here are a few reminders of what felt like some very testing times …

1   What did the remarkable escapes of 1977, against Bristol City, and 1997, against Tottenham, have in common?

2   How did Jimmy Hill incur the wrath of both Sunderland and the Football League in that infamous 1977 escape?

3   By the mid-1980s City took escapology to an art form. Can you name the three teams City had to beat in the three successive last-day clashes from 1984 to 1986, to preserve top-flight status?

4   In 1984, which future Sky Blues striker saw his last-minute header hit the inside of a post and bounce out when a goal would have relegated the Sky Blues?

5 In 1992 at Villa Park, which ex-Sky Blue scored one of the goals that defeated City 2–0 and left them praying that Notts County had beaten Luton (which they did!)?

6 City's sensational 2–1 at Tottenham in May 1997 secured their safety, but which star signing's two crosses set up strikes from Dion Dublin and Paul Williams?

7 After City's 2–1 miracle at White Hart Lane in 1997, what did *Match of the Day* pundit Alan Hansen declare Steve Ogrizovic had just done?

8 In the club's second season in the First Division (since rebranded the Championship) in 2002–03, Gary McAllister's men nosedived dreadfully after Christmas, taking them perilously close to the drop zone. After the Boxing Day win over Reading, how many league games did City win out of their final 21 fixtures?

9  On the final day of the 2007–08 season City were at it again, this time staying up despite a 4–1 defeat away to Charlton as other results went their way. Which loan keeper, who featured in the 2014–15 Premier League season, was badly at fault for 2 of the Charlton goals that so nearly sank the Sky Blues?

10  After that shocker at The Valley, which City boss declared, 'I'm delighted we have stayed up but not in the fashion we did. The players weren't celebrating in the dressing room. None of us were.'?

# Round
# 6

# Home from Home

For most of Coventry City's long and proud history, Highfield Road was home. Nothing lasts for ever though and in recent years, a bit like the Paul Young song once declared, it has almost become a matter of 'Wherever I lay my hat, that's my home!' See how well you know your own patch …

1   In how many different centuries did Coventry City play at Highfield Road?

2   What unwelcome hat-trick was completed at Highfield Road in the 1940s?

3   When Highfield Road was turned into an all-seater stadium in 1981, average attendances dropped by nearly 4,000 the next year. What happened to gate receipts that same year and why?

4   That whole heap of Highfield Road tradition finally ended
     in 2005 when City moved to the Ricoh Arena. For how
     many years had Highfield Road been the club's home?

5   When plans were first announced for 'Arena 2000',
     the plan was for the latest and smartest stadium design.
     Name two of the features that were originally planned
     for the stadium, but never materialised.

6   Highfield Road was not exclusively used to host football
     matches. Which of these events was *not* staged at the
     old ground: a Rod Stewart concert, a Jehovah's Witness
     convention, an Elton John concert or Real Ale festivals?

7   Which of these bits of Highfield Road memorabilia
     were not available to buy after City left Highfield Road:
     the floodlights, the goalposts, one square foot
     sections of the turf, stand seats, or the road sign for
     Highfield Road?

# GMK

### 🔵 GARY MABBUTT'S KNEE
**THE SKY BLUES FANZINE  EST1998  ISSUE48  APRIL2005**

# Bye, Bye, Highfield Road

**COVENTRY CITY FOO**
Season
**THE END OF AN ERA**
www.ccfc.co.uk
FOOTBALL
Email Address
ticket office@ccfc.co.uk

**£1**

**Part One of a GMK special**

**PLUS: STARBUCKS & THE NEW ARENA - CITY'S PLAYER AVALANCHE - ERNIE'S MATCH-FIXING CLAIMS - THE MIKE McGINNITY DIARIES - BEERS & CHEERS - AND MORE!**

8  Which prestigious international sport has the Ricoh hosted?

9  After eight years at the Ricoh Arena, club owners SISU relocated the club to Northampton due to a rent dispute. The season before the move, City averaged just under 11,000 per home game. To the nearest 100, what did they average in 2014, at Sixfields?

10  Finally, what was the sting in the tail awaiting City chiefs, just months after returning to the Ricoh?

# Round
# 7

# Over the Hill

While Coventry City fans are rightly proud of their longstanding
tradition of nurturing home-grown talent, it is fair to say that
there has been more than the odd occasion where the City
dressing room has included one or two more senior citizens.
Here come some of the best and worst …

1   A Cup Final hero from the 1960s, this diminutive striker
    wound down his playing career in the top flight at
    Highfield Road in the early '70s. Name him.

2   A huge favourite with Evertonians in the 1970s, by the
    time this striker stopped off at Highfield Road in the
    early '80s his once-feared goal-scoring powers were
    very much on the wane. Who was he?

3   This tough-as-teak stopper had lined up in a World Cup
    semi-final just months before jetting into Highfield Road
    in the early '90s. Who was he?

4   This record-breaking England international joined Ron
    Atkinson's playing staff in the mid-1990s. The closest he
    came to the first team was a place on the bench, before
    leaving to reach a fantastic milestone at Leyton Orient.
    Can you name him?

5   Which Scottish Braveheart briefly helped shore
    up the City backline in the 1999–2000 season of
    *The Entertainers*?

6   This Scottish international footballer and cricketer played
    briefly for City in their first season after dropping from
    the Premier League. Despite his advanced age, he could
    still (just about!) catch a ball. Who was he?

7   This straight-talking, tough-tackling Premier League
    winner was a marquee signing for manager Peter Reid.
    Sadly, he failed to dazzle. Who was he?

8   In a tumultuous 2002–03 season, Gary McAllister turned
    to an old Foxes team-mate to shore up his defence.
    The defensive strongman was found to be off the pace in
    his few outings in Sky Blue, who was he?

9   Eyebrows were raised when Mickey Adams brought
    Dennis Wise to the club in January 2006. Wise enjoyed
    a successful spell though, scoring 6 times and helping
    City to an eighth place finish, but how old was he?

10  In the relegation season of 2012, Andy Thorn turned
    to an Icelandic defender in his late thirties to bring
    experience to his left flank. Who was this one-time
    FA Cup winner who played only twice?

# Round

# 8

# Heading for the Exit

Hundreds of City stars have come and gone over the seasons, but not all leave when contracts expire or when form dips. The following key men headed for the exit in a variety of ways …

1  After leading the Sky Blues from Division Three to Division One, what was the job offer that Jimmy Hill received in 1967 that resulted in him leaving the Highfield Road hot seat?

2  Way back in 1984, after a disappointing home reverse against Stoke, what promise did City manager Bobby Gould make, and then keep, to keeper Raddy Avramović?

3  How many times has cup-winning coach John Sillett been sacked by the Sky Blues? And where was he when he was sacked on the last occasion?

4  In pre-season 1993, promising midfielder Lee Hurst
   sustained a career-ending injury in unusual
   circumstances – what were they?

5  Which 1998 star signing changed his mind over moving
   to Coventry? He opted instead for Madrid and left
   without once pulling on a first-team shirt.

6  In 2000, which Sunderland winger's challenge on Steve
   Froggatt led to the City winger's premature retirement?
   Interestingly, the Black Cat's man was never booked.

7  In May 2004, City sacked Eric Black a day after a
   memorable away game at Gillingham. What was the
   result of Black's final game in charge and what unique
   event happened down at Priestfield?

8  In 2010, a future international manager bade farewell
   to City on the back of an 11-game winless run and a
   final day 4–0 home reversal. Which proud patriot was
   immediately relieved of his duties?

9  In 2012, how did ex-midfielder Gary 'Pitbull' Deegan upset people shortly before leaving the club for Hibernian?

10 What took eight City players to Broad Street Rugby Club for training in 2013? Can you name them?

# Round
## 9

# One-hit Wonders

Players make lasting impressions for all sorts of reasons –
whether it is fantastic form or even comedy value.
The following players and staff may have only had fleeting
City careers, but they certainly made an impression …

1　Way back in the late 1970s, City youth keeper
Steve Murcott made his debut and only appearance
for the first team in very unlikely circumstances.
What were they?

2　In addition to just seven first-team outings, player-
manager Terry Butcher also made one appearance in
the 1991–92 Zenith Data Systems Cup competition.
What extraordinary exploit did Butcher register in
that match?

3　One of the brightest moments of Ron Atkinson's reign
was a 5–0 thrashing of then League Champions
Blackburn Rovers at a snowy Highfield Road in 1995.
Which City defender starred in his one and only match?

4   What made rock-hard frontman Mick Harford's solitary appearance in Sky Blue memorable in 1993?

5   In late 1999, which back-up Italian keeper was soon saying *arrivederci* after letting in 5 second-half goals in a League Cup tie at Tranmere?

6   In October 2000, rookie keeper Chris Kirkland was sent off at Stamford Bridge. Who was the replacement keeper who had to pick the ball out of his net six times in his only appearance for the Sky Blues?

7   Name the two men who temporarily took charge of first-team affairs in February 2008, in between the reins of Iain Dowie and Chris Coleman. The duo, one of whom was a former rugby league coach, oversaw a 0–0 home draw with Cardiff and a crushing 5–0 FA Cup reversal at home to West Brom.

8   Striker Roy O'Donovan was with City as a youth player and later re-signed for Aidy Boothroyd in 2010. In all his time with the club, he scored just once, in a 3–1 League Cup reversal – against which team?

9   In November 2013, this fleet-footed Jamaican forward
    was loaned from Premier League Norwich City. His stay
    was fleeting in the extreme; registering barely 10
    minutes in one goalless appearance from the bench
    against Notts County. Who was the mystery man?

10  During another loan spell in late 2013, forward-thinking
    midfielder Chris Maguire only started once for City,
    but did appear a couple of times from the bench. What
    made his substitute appearance at Milton Keynes hard
    to forget?

# Round

# 10

# Hat-trick Heroes

There can be few better sights for any football fans than seeing a favourite player hit a hat-trick. City fans have not been overwhelmed with such moments of glory, but here are a few to savour …

1  All-time leading scorer Clarrie Bourton starred for City in the 1930s. In his first season at Highfield Road how many hat-tricks did the deadly finisher rattle home?

2  At the end of the 1970s, burly striker Mick Ferguson recorded several trebles for the club. After one convincing home win over Ipswich Town, what Fergie-inspired message was put up on the scoreboard?

3   What was unusual about the 3 goals Garry Thompson
    scored in the thrilling 3–2 win over West Ham United
    in the 1981 League Cup semi-final?

4   Name the striker who marked his 1982 home debut with
    a treble against Everton.

5   What remarkable feat did David Speedie achieve
    in a 4–3 home reverse against Tony Mowbray's
    Middlesborough in 1988? Did he ever manage to repeat
    the trick?

6   Peter Ndlovu's superb treble against Liverpool in 1995
    was the first hat-trick scored by an opposing team at
    Anfield for how many years?

7   On the opening day of the 1997–98 season Dion Dublin
    notched all 3 City goals in an extraordinary 3–2 win.
    Which French defender did Dublin terrorise, just months
    before he went on to win a World Cup winner's medal?

8   Name the two teams Darren Huckerby scored hat-tricks
    against on successive Saturdays at Highfield Road in 1999.

9   Four City players have scored hat-tricks in the Premier
    League – Ndlovu, Dublin and Huckerby are three, but who
    was the other and also the first to achieve the feat?

10  In the early 2000s City recorded an 8–0 League Cup
    win over Rushden & Diamonds. Which up-and-coming
    striker bagged his only treble for the Sky Blues?

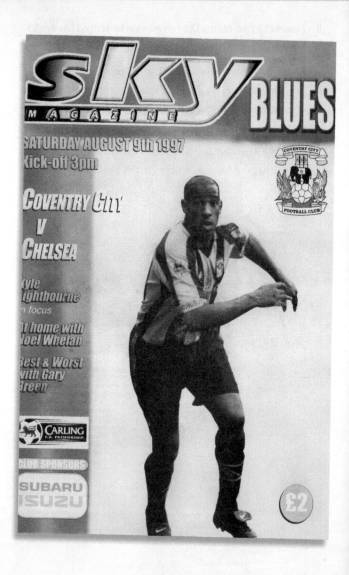

# Through the Ranks

For modern clubs with less financial muscle, the task of producing your own academy players has become more important than ever. Over many years Coventry City have launched plenty of future stars into the professional game; here are some reminders of the ones that stayed, and the ones that got away …

1   Which future European Cup winning captain began his football career as an apprentice at Coventry City, before chalking up almost 200 appearances in Sky Blue?

2   Which other member of that same European Cup winning squad also started his footballing life with the Sky Blues?

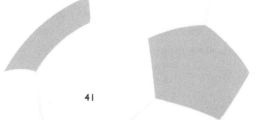

3   A highly rated academy striker first appeared for the Sky
    Blues in a famous 4–1 win at Villa Park in February 1999.
    Who was the precocious 16 year old who didn't touch
    the ball that day?

4   This capable and cultured central defender was
    considered an outstanding academy prospect.
    He debuted for City in their last Premiership
    appearance – a drab 0–0 draw against similarly
    relegated Bradford City. Who was he?

5   After City's relegation from the Premiership in 2001,
    which local stopper, who had learned his trade alongside
    Steve Ogrizovic and Magnus Hedman, was snapped up by
    Liverpool for a record-breaking £6 million?

6   In the mid-2000s, this talented forward-thinking academy
    prospect briefly seemed set for stardom. After a time
    though, off-field distractions slowed his progress and
    he finally went down the divisions after leaving City.
    Name the attack-minded midfielder.

7 On the opening day of the 2011–12 season, which 17-year-old ball-playing academy graduate did Andy Thorn surprisingly hand a debut to against Sven-Göran Eriksson's Leicester?

8 Which local youth team was Conor Thomas playing for when he was spotted by City scouts?

9 In 2013, this powerful City academy graduate was released by Steven Pressley after over fifty first-team outings. He moved to play for a load of Cobblers – who was he?

10 In the summer of 2014, which two shining lights from the City academy departed for high-flying Championship teams?

# Round
# 12

# Between the Sticks

Coventry have been lucky to have some fantastic keepers over the years, from Matthews and Glazier through to Ogrizovic and Westwood. The men in green (yellow, red or even lurid purple!) have given us many moments to remember and talk about afterwards!

1 City's oldest-ever player is Alf Wood, who played in goal for the first team in 1958 when he was employed as a trainer. How old was Wood when he stepped back into the limelight?

2 On a similar note, how old was Steve Ogrizovic when he bowed out of first-team action in 2000 against Sheffield Wednesday?

3 Which ex-TV presenter and expert conspiracy theorist is often famously described as a Coventry City goalkeeper, although he never played for the first team?

4 Which City keeper went to the 1978 World Cup with Scotland?

5 And who was his great rival at the club, who he alternated with in the late 1970s and early '80s?

6 In September 1989 a rare injury to Steve Ogrizovic away at Millwall catapulted which diminutive striker into the nets? How did he fare at The Den?

7 A City youth goalkeeper who played less than 10 senior games, this millennium man later gave up the game to professionally play another sport. Who was he, and which other sport did he go on to?

8 Which City skipper also had to deputise for the regular number 1 (then Ian Bennett) in 2005 against Stoke City? He played for almost an hour: how many goals did he concede?

9   In 2010, which City keeper became the first since 1987 to win the club's Player of the Year award?

10  Name the three keepers who played league matches for Coventry in 2014–15.

# Round

# 13

# **Debuts**

Even before a ball has been kicked, whenever any player makes his full debut for the first team, for minutes at least, an outpouring of goodwill can be felt. Everyone wishes the newcomer well, dreaming that the new addition might be just the missing ingredient the team has been looking for. Sadly though, just like with your list for Santa, not all our dreams come true …

1   After just one reserve appearance, which 16-year-old keeper made his debut against Southampton in 1982?

2   Which future cup winner debuted in defence in a 10-goal shocker at Southampton in 1984?

SKY BLUES

v. MAN UTD

Official Matchday Magazine of Coventry City F.C. Tues. 28th December 1982 k.o. 3.00 p.m.

30p

3   Which two full-backs, who would both go on to play prominent roles in the cup final team, both debuted on the opening day of the 1985–86 season?

4   Which City player must have felt like making a resolution not to play for the Sky Blues again, after making his first appearance in a New Year's Eve 4–0 thrashing by Spurs in 1994?

5   During the desperate spring of 1997, which Ukrainian was so shaken up on his debut at Old Trafford that he was subbed after just 30 minutes?

6   On the opening day victory against Portsmouth in 2010, which two players made their second 'debuts' for the Sky Blues?

7   In 2013, how did a nervous Ryan Haynes make his mark during his debut against Leyton Orient?

8 On the opening day of the 2014–15 season, what did Réda Johnson do on his debut that Robbie Keane and Mick Quinn had previously managed on their club debuts?

9 Staying with the present, how many debutants did Steven Pressley field on that opening day fixture at Bradford in August 2014?

10 In August 2015, Tony Mowbray handed debuts to four new signings for the season-opener against Wigan Athletic. Name the four men who started so promisingly.

# Round 14

# Bargain Basement

Apart from a brief spell towards the end of their Premier League days, Coventry have never been a club able to splash too much cash around. Instead, the Sky Blues have had to rely on young players, good scouting and hitting upon the odd uncut diamond …

1  In the autumn of 1983, Bobby Gould raided Wealdstone and picked up a promising defender for only £25,000. Who was he?

2  Who did City pay just £72,500 for in the summer of 1984?

3   That same summer, which man-mountain moved from Nottingham for £60,000?

4   Which speedy striker was spotted on a tour abroad and later flew into Highfield Road for just £10,000?

5   Name the ex-Halesowen Town forward, signed for £20,000, who scored on his debut on Boxing Day 1991 at Bramall Lane.

6   Which heroic City centre-back was earning his living from insurance while playing for Moor Green, when Terry Butcher signed him?

7   Although this frontman weighed in at a whopping £2 million, over 70 top-tier strikes and a resale value of almost £6 million made the initial fee seem like a snip. Who was he?

8   In late 1997, which young Dutchman was snapped up for just £220,000 from Dutch high-flyers Feyenoord?

9   In early 2007, City picked up an established international striker from Norway's Lillestrom. The striker buzzed around to great effect during his time in Sky Blue – who was he?

10  Which two Frenchmen, who achieved different levels of success at the club, signed up on free transfers in the summer of 2012?

# Round 15

# Big Mouths

From sublime strikes to catastrophic cock-ups, seasoned
City fans have experienced most things that football can
throw at them over the years. Of course the events on and
off the pitch are only part of the fun; listening to the players
and the pundits can sometimes be more entertaining than
the matches …

1  Name the highly regarded City defender who is talking
   and also who he is describing, '… can look scary
   sometimes, but he is such a nice fella. He's a gentle giant
   and was a great partner to play alongside.'

2  Which City hitman once had reason to say, 'To run up a
   score-line like this against the club who I idolised as a
   kid is so thrilling … I can't find the words'?

3  Which star of the late 1990s once declared, 'You want to
   go out and have a few beers with the lads, and situations
   will crop up and you just don't think'?

4  Who once said of whom, 'We would not be in the Premier League now if it wasn't for him'?

5  In his highly regarded 1998 book *Staying Up*, Warwick University academic and City-fan Rick Gekoski finished by telling one of the City first-teamers of the time, 'Watching you play is thrilling.' Who were the kind words for?

6  The lines, 'It doesn't matter if Manchester United come in with the money, I am happy to stay,' were uttered by which burly striker?

7  Which twenty-first-century City boss revealed of his time at the helm, 'Unfortunately, the project was not how it was sold to me and I felt that I could have achieved a lot more with the right support'?

8  Still in the 2000s, name the City boss who was not short on self-confidence when he declared, 'I help people help themselves, that is what I do. I listen to them, find out what gets them going and work on that.'

9 Which recent City manager finished his end of season programme notes by observing that, '... the rebuilding of any football club without a huge financial investment does not happen overnight'?

10 Can you name the very popular City player who took time to issue a statement to the fans when he left, including these lines: '... to captain a club of this size from where I have come from, fighting since the age of 16 to survive having nothing and earning £50 a week for years with a young child is amazing for me'?

# The League Cup

While City fans above a certain age can always point to
Wembley 1987, similar success has so far eluded the Sky
Blues in the other major cup competition, the League Cup.
There have still been plenty of moments to savour though …

1 Way back in 1965, City suffered their worst-ever home
   defeat in a quarter-final tie at home to local rivals
   Leicester. By how many did the Foxes win?

2 City's first major semi-final came in 1981 against
   West Ham. What fantastic comeback did Gordon
   Milne's men achieve in the first leg?

3 On the way to their 1990 semi-final, which City
   number 10 bagged 4 goals in a 5–0 quarter-final romp
   over Sunderland?

4 In that 1990 semi-final, which ex-City star scored the
   decisive goal for Forest?

5 The following season, City knocked out the holders of the previous two years, Nottingham Forest. The 9-goal thriller was one of Highfield Road's best-ever cup ties, but what was so unusual about the way the scoring went?

6 In 2007–08, City played that season's winners of the Champions League in the League Cup. What happened that night?

7 In 2008, City pushed a Premier League team all the way to extra-time at the Ricoh, before bowing out 3–2. It needed an England striker to score the winner – who was he, and who was he playing for that night?

8   When City lost 2–0 to Morecambe in a 2010 first-round League Cup tie, how many divisions lower were the Shrimps than City?

9   In August 2012, goals from Cody McDonald, Kevin Kilbane and Carl Baker saw the Sky Blues home in an extra-time thriller against Birmingham City. Who was City's manager that night?

10  The following month, September 2012, Mark Robbins' first away game in charge came in a glamour tie at the Emirates. How many did City lose by that night and who scored a rare goal for them?

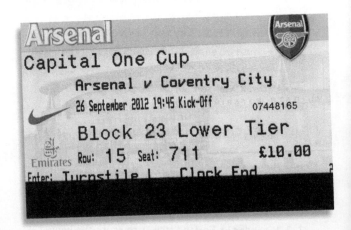

**Round**

**17**

# The 1987 FA Cup

16 May 1987 was an unforgettable day, bursting with brilliant memories. Enjoy reminding yourself of some of them ...

1  Which City midfield enforcer celebrated his 100th first-team appearance in the 1987 Cup Final?

2  A year before soaring across the Wembley turf to score one of the FA Cup's most memorable headers, how did Keith Houchen spend Cup Final day 1986?

3  Why did Coventry fans take to singing, 'Are you watching Jimmy Greaves' as the cup run progressed?

4  Where did John Sillett and George Curtis take the team away to before big cup ties, and why?

5  Who was the only City player from the 1987 final who had previously played in an FA Cup Final, and how had he fared?

OFFICIAL MATCH MAGAZINE                    £1.00

**COVENTRY CITY v LEEDS UNITED**

# THE FINAL GOAL

**F.A. CUP SEMI-FINAL**
at Hillsborough Sheffield on
Sunday 12th April 1987, kick-off 12.15 p.m.

6   As a sign of the times of British football in the 1980s, most City players were home-grown. Name the only non-English player in City's thirteen-man squad.

7   Name all 5 of Keith Houchen's goals on the cup run.

8   Where did Brian Borrows have to watch the final? Why?

9   In what colourful way did the council help the celebrations in Coventry city centre the night of the Cup Final victory?

10   An enormous crowd greeted the cup winners the next day on an open-top bus ride through the streets of Coventry. What was the reported size of the crowd?

# The Dreaded Drop

In 2001 and again in 2012, Coventry suffered relegations from the top two tiers of English football. After a proud thirty-four-year run of top-flight football, City fans have had a lot to get used to, and all because of these events …

1  After being brought in as a replacement for Milan-bound Robbie Keane, how many goals did £6 million striker Craig Bellamy score in his only season at the club?

2  Which hefty striker, who joined late in the 2001 season, briefly looked like his goals might help pull off another remarkable escape?

3  As sometimes happens late in the season, a former Coventry star came back to score a crucial goal against them. Which treble-winning red curled in a fantastic free-kick to all but seal relegation for the Sky Blues?

4  At which ground were City relegated?

5  What were the words on the home-made banner that one fan defiantly held aloft when relegation was confirmed?

6  After eleven years in the Championship, Andy Thorn's 2012 vintage suffered the same sinking feeling. Despite faltering form all season, what formation did Thorn persist with that failed to dazzle?

7  What unwelcome card did Gäel Bigirimana receive on his eighteenth birthday?

8  After Christmas, leading scorer Lukas Jutkiewicz left the club and was replaced by loanee Alex Nimely. How many goals did each player notch that season?

# THE Pink

COVENTRY EVENING TELEGRAPH, SATURDAY, MAY 5, 2001     32p

# ARCH ENEMIES VILLA PUT THE BOOT IN AS SKY BLUES ARE RELEGATED

# DOWN

### TODAY'S RESULTS

| | | |
|---|---|---|
| Aston Villa | | 3 |
| Sky Blues | | 2 |
| Man Utd | | 0 |
| Derby County | | 1 |
| Bradford City | | 1 |
| Middlesbrough | | 1 |

**FA CARLING PREMIERSHIP**

| | P | W | D | L | F | A | P | GD |
|---|---|---|---|---|---|---|---|---|
| Everton | 37 | 11 | 8 | 18 | 43 | 57 | 41 | -14 |
| Derby | 37 | 10 | 11 | 16 | 35 | 56 | 41 | -20 |
| Middlesbro | 37 | 8 | 15 | 14 | 42 | 43 | 39 | -1 |
| Man City | 36 | 8 | 10 | 18 | 39 | 61 | 34 | -22 |
| Sky Blues | 37 | 8 | 9 | 20 | 36 | 63 | 33 | -27 |
| Bradford | 35 | 5 | 10 | 20 | 29 | 62 | 25 | -33 |

**EARLY DOORS:** Moustapha Hadji celebrates his first goal at Villa Park today

**By ANDY TURNER**

GORDON STRACHAN's Sky Blues went down fighting today as they were relegated to the first division – bringing an end to 34 years of top flight football.

Despite City getting off to a dream start with two spectacular first-half goals from Moustapha Hadji the visitors simply couldn't hold onto their lead against Midland rivals Aston Villa.

### Killer

Substitute David Ginola led the charge and Darius Vassell pulled a goal back early after the break before Juan Pablo Angel scored the killer equaliser with nine minutes to go, signalling the end of City's Premiership status.

Paul Merson then smashed home the winner four minutes later to hammer the final nail in the coffin at the worst possible venue for the fans who were left to applaud their team off the field and contemplate life in the Nationwide League.

**INSIDE: FOUR-PAGE SCHOOLS FOOTBALL FINALS PULL-OUT**

9 What did City do against Middlesbrough in January 2012 that they did not do in any other game that season?

10 After the turn of the year, City won 5 out of 6 home matches, which gave them hope of avoiding the drop. Their away form remained dreadful though: how many away games did they win all year?

# Round 19

# Make the Link

Over the years, City fans have seen their favourites make headlines for all sorts of reasons, from footballing feats to some notorious capers. This selection of unlikely pairings, each featuring at least one City star, is bound together in some unusual ways – can you make the links?

1  First man on the moon Neil Armstrong and City's own high-flyer – mascot Sky Blue Sam.

2  Original Iron Man George Curtis and original bad-boy David Speedie.

3  Recently retired England captain Steven Gerrard and City's own home-grown enforcer, Conor Thomas.

4 England's record outfield caps holder David Beckham and City's ex-skipper, tricky winger, Carl Baker.

5 Liverpool legend and one-time Real Madrid galactico, Michael Owen, and City's leading top-flight scorer, Dion Dublin.

6 One-time City striker Cody McDonald and *X Factor* runner-up Olly Murs.

7 Record appearance maker for the Sky Blues, Steve Ogrizovic, and record appearance maker for Manchester United, Ryan Giggs.

8 All-time great Sir Stanley Matthews and three very capable goalkeepers in Steve Ogrizovic, Peter Shilton and John Lukic share an almost unbelievable feat. What can it be?

9 World-famous guitarist David Evans and City's French central defender William Edjenguélé who played over 30 games in the 2012–13 season.

10 City midfielder ball player Adam Barton and some monkeys from Sheffield.

# Round

# 20

# The Bosses

City supremoes have come in all shapes and sizes over the years: from the tactically astute to the more hair-brained. Sadly, the top men in recent decades have not been able to hit upon the magic that the likes of Sillett and Hill provided.

1 Name four player-managers of the last twenty-five years.

2 Which of those player-managers is, so far, the only first-team manager to have been sent off while playing for the first team?

3 List three other managers of the last thirty years who played for City before they ever managed them.

4 Iain Dowie's reign at the Ricoh was short-lived – just twelve months. However, in that time he masterminded memorable cup victories against two top-flight teams. Name the teams City turned over.

5 Although sacking a manager just before the end of a season is a bit like bolting the gate after the horse has gone, different City boards have been known to do just this. Name the late season casualties of 2002 and 2004.

6 Which famous pairing took charge of the final fixture of 2002 for 1 match only?

7   Which manager of the 2000s managed Real Sociedad in
    Spain's Second Division, before signing on at the Ricoh?

8   What position did Aidy Boothroyd take City to when they
    entertained Leeds United in November 2010?

9   Before taking over first-team affairs, what was Andy
    Thorn's role at the club?

10  Stability was lacking in the 2012–13 season as City
    galloped through five first-team mangers of one sort or
    other. Name the five men who took on the reins.

# Who am I?

See if you can work out who these significant figures from City's past and present are, with the help of just a few unlikely clues …

1  I signed from Blackburn for £750.
   I loved trebles.
   I'm still top of the pile.

2  I used to watch on the Spion Kop.
   I starred for my boyhood team.
   I managed my boyhood team.

3  I worked at, and played for, Snowden Colliery in Kent.
   I started as a Bantam, and became a Sky Blue.
   I played in all four divisions.

4  I scored a memorable bicycle kick.
   I partnered a big man.
   I brought in lots of pennies.

5  I was a Toffee, then a Trotter.
   I timed my tackles like quartz time their watches.
   Injury robbed me of my biggest day.

6 I cost a million, but stayed a decade.
  I helped a Frenchman fly.
  I scored every 298 games.

7 I sound cross.
  I am in the top ten international scorers of all time.
  I scored in a memorable finale in 2005.

8 I broke records in the youth team.
  I debuted in a massacre at Villa Park.
  I have been a Hatter, a Bluenose and an Iron.

9 My uncle was a goal-scoring Canary.
  I played for a famous first team at 15.
  I am known for my passing.

10 While wearing Sky Blue, I saw red.
   I was known for my physical presence.
   I worked when things were 'far from ideal'.

# Round

# 22

# Spot Kicks

Whenever the referee points to the spot, cries of anguish sit alongside hushed anticipation in equal measure. Like all fans, City followers have had their share of memorable and miserable moments from 12 yards out …

1   Which City keeper famously saved from Liverpool's Phil Neal in a 1978 victory over the reigning European champions?

2   Coventry had to beat Stoke City to keep alive their chances of avoiding the drop in 1985. With minutes to go, Stoke were awarded a spot kick – what happened?

3   A year after the Cup Final win over Spurs, Coventry
    nearly returned to Wembley again. They lost 4–3 in a
    semi-final shoot-out to second-division Reading, but
    what was the competition they were in?

4   Which City stopper missed against soon-to-be champions
    Arsenal in 1989, only to convert a second decisive kick
    80 minutes later?

5   How did Mick Quinn manage to hit a penalty out of the
    ground when he blazed over against Newcastle United
    in 1993?

6   Name two of the three players who missed penalties for
    City in their FA Cup quarter-final shoot-out defeat
    against Sheffield United in 1998?

7   In the same shoot-out, who was in goal for City,
    and how many kicks did he save?

8   In the first round of the 2013 Johnstone's Paint Trophy, after a fairly dire 0–0 match against Burton Albion, City squeezed through a marathon shoot-out. How many spot kicks were taken before City secured their place in the next round?

9   Which unlikely figure scored the winning penalty against Burton?

10  Over two seasons, 2013–14 and 2014–15, name six different players who missed from the spot for the Sky Blues.

# Big Mouth Strikes Again!

As all football fans know only too well, players, managers and pundits are all as capable of producing hot air as each other. While the search for enlightening and incisive comments can sometimes be a long and fruitless one, at least City fans have heard plenty of lines to smirk at …

1  An all-time City great was once described by his manager as being the 'strongest man in the blessed world'. Who said the line and about whom?

2  When and why did City boss John Sillett declare that the club was going to start 'shopping at Harrods in future'?

3  How did master-of-mirth Ron Atkinson get the Sky Blues into an often-repeated quip about the *Titanic*?

4   Gordon Strachan declared one of his City talents was
    a 'world beater one week', but 'a carpet beater'
    the next. Which erratic young English talent was
    Strachan describing?

5   'You can sit there and play with all your silly machines
    as much as you like … if the boys haven't done enough,
    I'll whip 'em.' Which Sky TV pundit benefitted from that
    tetchy post-match analysis from which City boss?

6   A one-time star striker at Highfield Road in the
    Premier League declared in his autobiography, 'I never
    once enjoyed it at Coventry, the players were a great
    bunch of lads, but the ground (Highfield Road) was
    poor.' Name this pantomime villain.

7   'I thought I was Superman after what I had done at …
    but I soon realised I couldn't be Superman every day,'
    was the interesting observation made by which City
    manager of the 2000s (if you're not sure take a guess –
    it could be one of a dozen!)?

8 Which City boss of the 2010s put everyone's mind at rest, just weeks before he left, with the following assurance: 'Opportunities will come and opportunities will go, but I'm not going anywhere.'

9 According to the newspaper reports, before becoming involved with the Sky Blues, a leading light behind the SISU scene was once, surprisingly, accused of having 'balls of steel'. Who was that ballsy fighter?

10 Name the recent City boss who declared in a post-match interview: 'As for my own personal performance, I have to apologise. I was a bit caught up in the game and got emotional. I felt there were decisions not going our way, but I need to behave better than I did today.'

# Take Your Pick!

Be careful – the following City conundrums have more red herrings than the Atlantic, the Baltic and the Pacific oceans put together …

1   In the Sky Blues' only European campaign so far, in 1970, did …

   *David Icke save a penalty*        *City lose a penalty shoot-out*

   *City lose 6–1 in                    City beat*
   *the Bernabéu*                      *Bayern Munich 2–1*

2   Which ex-City chairman once scored two first-class hundreds for Warwickshire in the same match?

   *Tim Fisher*                          *Geoffrey Robinson*

   *Jimmy Hill*                          *Bryan Richardson*

3  Under the brief stewardship of Done Howe in 1992, the Sky Blues set a new club record of ...

Four successive 0–0 draws        Nine successive defeats

9 games without a goal        Four successive sendings off

4  Within twenty-four months of being sacked by Coventry in the mid-1980s, Bobby Gould ...

Hosted a daytime
TV show

Opened a pub on
Gosford Street

Managed Wales        Won the FA Cup

5  What was ex-City chief Iain Dowie's master's degree in?

Media studies        Archaeology

Engineering        Travel and tourism

6  Before he became a professional footballer with Liverpool, Steve Ogrizovic ...

*Was a security guard*          *Was a policeman*

*Was a long-jump champion*      *Was a semi-pro basketball player*

7  After he retired from professional football, striker Mick Quinn worked ...

*Training greyhounds*           *As a chef*

*Training horses*               *As a PE teacher in a Coventry school*

8  During his successful spell at Highfield Road, which of the following did Dion Dublin *not* achieve ...

*Top scorer for four years*     *An England call-up*

*Winning the Golden Boot*       *A hit record with Showaddywaddy*

9 After City favourite Carl Baker left the club in 2014, he attracted some media attention for his new commute to work at Milton Keynes. Was he …

Power walking

Travelling in on his canal boat

Driving his Lamborghini

Biking to Tile Hill and getting the train

10 Between the two seasons, 2013–14 and 2014–15, how many loan players did City use?

Six

Twenty-six

Thirty-six

Sixteen

# Would You Believe It?

The weird and occasionally wonderful world of following Coventry City does, as Eurovision winner Dana once put it, throw up all kinds of everything. Here are some reminders of the very rich Sky Blue tapestry, from the bizarre to the downright ridiculous ...

1 How did Ernie Hunt manage to change the rules of football in 1970?

2 Why was a City strip, dating from the early 1980s, banned from television?

3 Why did City director Ted Stocker have 50,000 reasons to be cheerful in 1987?

4 While managing the Sky Blues, Gordon Strachan hit the headlines for non-football-related matters involving a Warwickshire bus and some big mouths. What was the 'Wee Man' up to?

5  How did local lad Chris Kirkland make his dad's dreams come true when he gained his only England cap against Greece in 2006?

6  Which masked outlaw starred for City in their run to the FA Cup quarter-finals in 2009?

7  How did a pint of milk kick-start Gäel Bigirimana's Coventry career?

8  How did the club's Head of Football Operations cause a stir in late 2011 by just sitting down?

9 They say lightning never strikes twice, but in City's case, for three successive mid-season transfer windows, disaster kept on striking. What damage was done to City's mid-season plans in 2011, 2012 and 2013?

10 What couldn't Tony Mowbray find at the football club in March 2015?

# Round 26

# The Numbers Game

For the statistically minded, numbers can be used to prove or disprove all sorts of things. Take a look at some of these amazing and alarming digits and see if you can make any sense of these Sky Blue stats …

1   Since forming in 1883, how many times have City been crowned champions of any division?

2   Clarrie Bourton enjoyed a record-breaking first season in 1931–32. He notched several hat-tricks on his way to how many goals?

3   Midfielder Ronnie Farmer famously played for City in all four divisions through the 1950s and '60s. During that time he took 23 penalties, how many did he score?

4   Steve Ogrizovic once went five years, from August 1984
    to September 1989, without missing a game. How many
    consecutive matches did he play?

5   The record transfer fee paid by City was splashed out
    in the summer of 2000 on striker Craig Bellamy. How
    much did the 8-goal striker cost?

6   Since the 1969–70 finish of sixth, which brought European
    football to the club, how many seasons in the last forty-
    five years have City spent in the top six of any division?

7   Gordon Strachan's 1999–2000 vintage received lots of
    plaudits for their attacking verve, which saw some great
    stuff played by McAllister, Hadji and Keane. In that same
    season, how many times did City win away from home
    in the league?

8   Richard Shaw signed for City in November 1995 and
    then went on a goal-scoring drought that lasted almost
    nine years. How many games did it take Shaw to break
    his duck, before he finally belted home a beauty away
    at Gillingham?

9 Four City players have played for England while on the books at Highfield Road – one in the 1950s, two in the '80s and one in the '90s. Can you name the four stars?

10 How many miles is Northampton's Sixfields ground from the Ricoh Arena?

**Round**

**27**

# Absent Friends

After leaving Coventry, it is surprising to see how far and wide some ex-City players can get to. While some have found that the grass can be greener in other climes, by no means all have. Some old-boys have gone on to make their marks in new and unexpected ways …

1 Name the two ex-City strikers who now talk for a living on a popular national radio station.

2 Name the City left-back from the 1980s who forged out a new career with some other boys in blue.

3 Which ex-City trialist (he was rejected) scored a 1987 hit with the memorable 'Diamond Lights' ditty that also featured another top international?

4 Name the ex-City midfielder who, after he retired, carried on his excellent delivery in his new walk of life.

# COVENTRY CITY

COVENTRY CITY
FOUNDED 1883
FOOTBALL CLUB

HOME    AWAY
COVENTRY CITY

COVENTRY CITY

**CLUB INFO:**
FOUNDED: 1883
NICKNAME: THE SKY BLUES
MANAGER: AIDY BOOTHROYD

## 3 KEY FIXTURES
● Leicester / Away / 26.02.11
● Nottingham Forest / Home / 01.02.
● Watford / Home / 02.04.11

**STADIUM STATS:**
Name:     Ricoh Arena
Capacity: 32,604
Address:  Phoenix Way,
          Coventry, CV6 6GE
Website:  www.ccfc.co.uk

Long throw legend Aron Gunnarsson had to decide between handball and football! He
went for football because it paid better but his handball playing dad wasn't happy!

**1**
GOALKEEPER
HEIGHT: 1.88m
D.O.B. 23/10/1984
KEIREN WESTWOOD

**2**
DEFENDER
HEIGHT: 1.80m
D.O.B. 11/8/1986
RICHARD KEOGH

**15**
DEFENDER
HEIGHT: 1.85m
D.O.B. 28/9/1986
MARTIN CRANIE

**20**
DEFENDER
HEIGHT: 1.90m
D.O.B. 21/8/1988
BEN TURNER

**24**
DEFENDER
HEIGHT: 1.83m
D.O.B. 5/7/1985
RICHARD WOOD

**4**
MIDFIELDER
HEIGHT: 1.80m
13/1/1984
SAMMY CLINGAN

**5**
MIDFIELDER
HEIGHT: 1.80m
28/2/1974
LEE CARSLEY

**7**
MIDFIELDER
HEIGHT: 1.78m
21/1/1984
DAVID BELL

5   Which ex-City hardman briefly reappeared in the
    Sky Sports spotlight, competing with other past and
    present pros at arm-wrestling?

6   After tough times at both Coventry and then Sunderland,
    which ex-City manager took time out of football to run
    a hotel in Scotland (he has since successfully returned)?

7   Which ex-City striker is now forging out a new career on
    the property renovation show, *Homes under the Hammer*?

8   Name the City midfielder from the 2000s who has gone
    on to clean up everything around him since retiring.

9   Name the ex-City striker from the 2000s who, since
    retiring from the game, has re-emerged in the boxing
    ring – where he is following in some family footsteps.

10  In a similar vein, name the strapping centre-back from
    the 2010s who took up detective work when he gave
    up football.

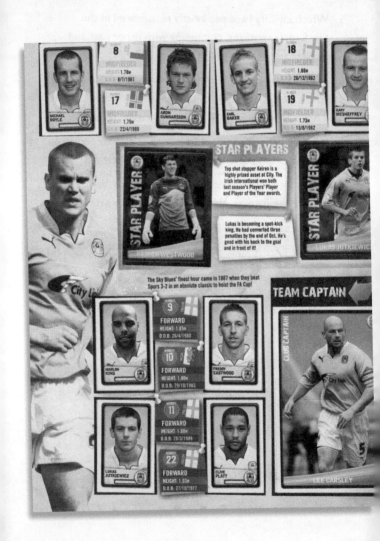

MICHAEL DOYLE

8
MIDFIELDER
HEIGHT: 1.78m
D.O.B. 8/7/1981

17
MIDFIELDER
HEIGHT: 1.75m
D.O.B. 22/4/1969

ARON GUNNARSSON

CARL BAKER
MIDFIELDER
HEIGHT: 1.88m
D.O.B. 28/12/1982

19
MIDFIELDER
HEIGHT: 1.73m
D.O.B. 13/8/1982

GARY McSHEFFREY

## STAR PLAYERS

Top shot stopper Keiren is a highly prized asset at City. The Irish international won both last season's Players' Player and Player of the Year awards.

Lukas is becoming a spot-kick king. He had converted three penalties by the end of Oct. He's good with his back to the goal and in front of it!

KEIREN WESTWOOD

STAR PLAYER

LUKAS JUTKIEWICZ

STAR PLAYER

The Sky Blues' finest hour came in 1987 when they beat Spurs 3-2 in an absolute classic to hoist the FA Cup!

## TEAM CAPTAIN

MARLON KING

9
FORWARD
HEIGHT: 1.85m
D.O.B. 26/4/1980

FREDDY EASTWOOD

10
FORWARD
HEIGHT: 1.80m
D.O.B. 29/10/1983

LUKAS JUTKIEWICZ

11
FORWARD
HEIGHT: 1.88m
D.O.B. 20/3/1989

CLIVE PLATT

22
FORWARD
HEIGHT: 1.93m
D.O.B. 27/10/1977

CLUB CAPTAIN

LEE CARSLEY

# Round

# 28

# **Premier League**

Sadly, many Sky Blues' fans have had to grow up with no memories of the (sometimes) heady top-flight days. Until the glory days come back, the best bet for the younger generations of fans is probably YouTube …

1 After three games of the opening Premier League season, where did City lie in the table?

2 What was the half-time entertainment in the first live Premier League game at Highfield Road in September 1992?

3  Which larger-than-life City manager could often be seen sporting sunglasses, whatever the weather, and even at night matches?

4  What was the common phrase used to describe that same boss's departure?

5  What striking City strip debuted in a 5–1 mauling at Ewood Park?

6  On a tense last day of the 1996 season, how did the then Manchester City manager, Alan Ball, inadvertently play a big part in keeping the Sky Blues up?

7  After not starting a game all season, Gordon Strachan returned to the City ranks in April 1997 against Chelsea. He gave a man-of-the-match performance in a 3–1 win over a Chelsea outfit that included Vialli, Zola and Hughes. How old was Strachan when he played that night?

8 In 1998, alongside Michael Owen, Dion Dublin was the Premiership joint top scorer. How many league goals did each player grab?

9 In August 1999, Robbie Keane became the Sky Blues' record signing at £6 million. Just a year later, how much was he sold for, and who did he go to?

10 Apart from Keane, name three other players whose departures in the summer of 2000 left City short of goals and experience, leading to the 2001 relegation.

# Countdown

Congratulations if your head has not yet imploded into a ball of Sky Blue mush, well done, you've nearly made it! The next section is filled with lists of all manner of Sky Blue matters, and they might just drive you to distraction …

10  Name the ten outfield players who started the 1987 FA Cup Final for City.

9  Name nine full-time permanent managers City have had since their 2001 relegation from the Premier League.

8 List eight full-time permanent managers City had during their thirty-four top-flight years.

7 Name seven different left-backs of the 2010s.

6 List six different goalkeepers of the 2010s.

5 Name five different African players who have played for Coventry (think Morocco, Zimbabwe …).

4 Excluding Wembley, name the four other grounds City played at during their 1987 cup run.

3 In three successive years, from 1999–2001, City smashed the £5 million mark to buy players. Who were those three star signings?

2 After Steve Ogrizovic on 601 matches, the next two top appearance makers for Coventry played in 538 and 492 games, from the 1950s to the 1980s. Who were the two outstanding club servants?

1 In 1996, one City star broke all the rules by refusing to leave the pitch after being sent off in a reserve game – who was the villain?

# Round

# 30

# **What Happened Next?**

A bit like a famous TV sports quiz, we thought it might be fun to finish with some more rekindled memories of the good, the bad and the sometimes ugly …

1 On Valentine's Day 1998, Gavin Strachan's sweeping cross-field ball was chested down by the advancing George Boateng who rode three challenges before shooting low to Mark Bosnich's right.
*What happened next?*

2 After a couple of unsavoury incidents on nights out, a talented City striker of the 1990s was told he was going to get a new address.
*What happened next?*

3  Just before Christmas 2002, City fans enjoyed a sparkling
   3–0 home win against Derby. Gary McAllister opened
   the scoring with one of the sweetest volleys ever seen at
   Highfield Road.
   *What happened next?*

4  In April 2005, a left-wing cross was not dealt with by the
   Derby defence, the ball bounced out to the edge of
   the area …
   *What happened next?*

5  In August 2012, Coventry let a 2–0 half-time lead
   slip against Bury. Despite the disappointing 2–2 draw,
   the Sky Blues were unbeaten in their first 4 games of
   the new season.
   *What happened next?*

6  In March 2013, with the Sky Blues losing 2–0 at home to
   Colchester United, substitute Callum Wilson chased
   the ball down the right flank.
   *What happened next?*

# SKY BLUE CUP FINAL

EVENING TELEGRAPH    18p    Saturday, May 16, 1987

**Coventry City 3 Tottenham Hotspur 2** *(after extra time)*

## Sky Blue heroes – to a man

**Neville Foulger sums up**

THEY'VE done it — George and John they've done it!

The magnificent Coventry City side motioned and motivated by George Curtis and John Sillett won the FA Cup in a Wembley classic today.

There have not been any better first halves in recent cup finals with both City and Spurs living up to all the pre-match promises and expectations.

The assault was on back and free flowing football and John Sillett's forecast that there could be few offside proved absolutely accurate.

It was lovely stuff to watch for the committed

**Turn to Back Page**

## Re-live the action with the

**Evening Telegraph**

24-PAGE COLOUR SOUVENIR ON SALE MONDAY — ONLY 30p

More bright and breezy reports and pictures in Monday's normal edition's

AND DON'T FORGET YOUR

PINK EXTRA TONIGHT

# Wembley wonders

Keith Houchen — man of the moment again as he dives to head in City's second equaliser to stun Spurs today

7   On Friday, 5 September 2014, the Sky Blues made
an emotional and triumphant return to the Ricoh.
The highly charged night was watched by 27,306 fans.
Eight days later, Yeovil Town visited the Ricoh.
*What happened next?*

8   After 40 minutes play opposing Worcester City, right-back
George Williams hurled a high throw into the City
penalty area which was routinely collected by Lee Burge.
*What happened next?*

9   In January 2015, City faced a typically busy few days.
City's U21s lined up at Sheffield United on the Monday
afternoon before the first team took on high-flying
Swindon, to be followed by an FA Youth Cup away tie at
Manchester City two days later.
*What happened next?*

10  John Motson once had reason to mutter these
words: 'This is Graham Rodger. Did that beautifully.'
The memorable match was played on a sunny afternoon
in London, a footballing lifetime ago.
*What happened next?*

THE ANSWERS

1 Ghanaian striker, Nii Lamptey.
2 Mo Konjic.
3 Aron Gunnarsson.
4 Youssef Chippo and Mustapha Hadji.
5 Viorel Moldovan scored for Romania in their 2–1 win over England.
6 Ysrael Zúñiga.
7 Clayton Ince and Stern John.
8 Michael Mifsud.
9 Claus Jørgensen.
10 Peter Ndlovu.

# Banana Skins

1 Soon-to-be manager Jimmy Hill.
2 Barrie Williams was an English teacher.
3 'It's the everlasting *teamwork* of every bloomin' soul.'
4 Matthew Hanlan was a bricklayer.
5 They would have to read the newspaper reports.
6 City were fourth in Division One (the top flight!).
7 Burge was playing in his fifth first-team match.
8 He kicked out at an opponent.
9 Johnson missed a penalty to equalise before half-time.
10 'Certain players are in a *comfort zone* and they'll be *gone from this* football club.'

1 There was no Sky Blue beer and chips.
2 John Sillett is the only one not to have watched his son play for City – his son, Neil, was physio for a time. Bobby Gould watched Jonathan Gould, Dave Phillips saw Aaron Phillips and Gordon Strachan saw Gavin and Craig Strachan both play.
3 Phil Babb was the only one who did not come to City from Everton.
4 Steve Froggatt was selected for an England squad while at City, but, unlike the other three, did not play for England.
5 Keiren Westwood did not come through the academy.
6 Woking are the only one of the four non-league teams to not knock City out. City beat the non-leaguers in 1997 – but only after a replay!
7 Jaguar Cars have not had a shirt sponsorship with City – the others all have.
8 Magnus Hedman is the odd one out as the other ex-City players all won over 100 international caps.
9 A gipsy curse!
10 Jim O'Brien was a rare permanent signing in a season of many loan players.

# Glory Days

1 Terry Gibson (4–0 home win December 1983) and Peter Ndlovu (3–2 away win March 1995).
2 Cyrille Regis headed home a Greg Downs cross.
3 Bobby Gould.
4 Everton were the recently crowned league champions who had also just won the European Cup Winners Cup. The significance of the result was that it completed City's remarkable escape from relegation – Norwich had ended their fixtures 8 points ahead of the Sky Blues, leaving City needing to win each of their last 3 games to overtake the Canaries in order to stay up, which they did!
5 Five times in an unlikely 5–0 win.
6 They scored less – Dublin and Huckerby hit 38 goals between them.
7 Huckerby's goal secured a 3–2 win, and City had been trailing 2–1 with just 4 minutes left.
8 Gary McAllister, Mustapha Hadji and Robbie Keane.
9 Dion Dublin with 61 league strikes (72 in total).
10 Danny Thomas, Cyrille Regis and Dion Dublin.

# Narrow Escapes

1 In each case, City's game was delayed kicked off after all the other fixtures – crowd congestion in 1977 and traffic problems in 1997. In theory this could have given the City players an advantage because they would have known exactly what score was needed to survive.

2 The decisive Sunderland result that night – a defeat at Everton – was flashed up on the scoreboard, thereby allowing both teams to play out the closing minutes with no intention of trying to score another goal. The 2–2 draw with Bristol City kept both teams up, but the manner in which the game ended was highly controversial.

3 The three narrow escapes, all at Highfield Road, were:
   1984 – Norwich 2–1
   1985 – Everton 4–1
   1986 – QPR 2–1

4 Robert Rosario.

5 Cyrille Regis scored in the first minute.

6 Gary McAllister.

7 With spiralling Premiership finances in mind, Hansen declared that each of two crucial late stops made by Ogrizovic had saved City £10 million each, as relegation would have cost the club £20 million.

8 One win only – a 2–0 win over Grimsby in March.

9 Kasper Schmeichel.

10 Chris Coleman.

# Home
# from Home

1 Three centuries – from 1899–2005.
2 The stadium was hit by bombs three times during hostilities in the Second World War.
3 Despite the crowds dropping so much, gate receipts went up 15 per cent. City's steep price increases allowed the club to gain financially from their dwindling attendances.
4 106 years.
5 A retractable roof, 40,000 seats and a sliding pitch were all in the original plans.
6 There was no Rod Stewart concert.
7 The road sign for Highfield Road is still on Highfield Road!
8 In the summer of 2012, the Ricoh hosted men's and women's international Olympic football.
9 Average gates at Sixfields were a paltry 2,570, a drop of a massive 77 per cent on the previous year's figure.
10 Wasps RFC coming in on the blind side to purchase the Ricoh.

1 Liverpool legend Ian St John.
2 Bob Latchford.
3 Terry Butcher.
4 Peter Shilton.
5 Colin Hendry.
6 Goalkeeper Andy Goram.
7 Tim Sherwood.
8 Steve Walsh.
9 Wise was 38.
10 Hermann Hreidarsson.

# Heading for the Exit

1 Working for London Weekend Television.
2 Gould vowed to never play Avramović again after a disappointing 2–3 reversal at home to Stoke – and he never did.
3 Sillett was sacked twice, in 1984 and 1990. Second time around, he was ill at home.
4 The very promising Hurst suffered a career-wrecking knee injury at the Sky Blues pre-season army training camp!
5 Croatian left-back Robert Jarni.
6 Nicky Summerbee.
7 In Black's last match in charge, Coventry won 5–2 away at Gillingham and Richard Shaw scored his first goal for the club after nine years and 298 appearances.
8 Chris Coleman.
9 Deegan posted inappropriate comments on Twitter about an Irish republican group.
10 In a move believed to be more to do with finances than form, City boss Steven Pressley deemed eight first-team squad members surplus to requirements. The 'bombsquad' were: Gary McSheffrey, William Edjenguélé, Steve Jennings, Cody McDonald, David Bell, Chris Dunn, Kevin Malaga and Jordan Clarke.

# Round 9 One-hit Wonders

1 Murcott was called on to make his only first-team outing when regular keeper Jim Blyth injured his knee in the warm-up.

2 Terry Butcher achieved the unique feat of becoming the first (and still the only) player-manager to be sent off while playing for the first team. Butcher was dismissed in a 2–0 home defeat against Aston Villa.

3 Ex-Arsenal defender Chris Whyte enjoyed his only Sky Blues appearance against Rovers.

4 In his only 15 minutes for City, Harford headed home the winner.

5 Italian keeper Raffaele Nuzzo.

6 The on-loan goalie was Alan Miller.

7 John Harbin and Frank Bunn.

8 O'Donovan's solitary strike was in a 3–1 defeat against Bury in the League Cup first round in August 2011.

9 Jamar Loza.

10 Maguire scored two free-kicks from outside the penalty area in front of thousands of jubilant away fans.

# Hat-trick Heroes

1 Bourton scored seven hat-tricks in his first season, 1931–32, including five trebles, one 4-goal haul and one 5-goal haul.

2 After Ferguson's 4-goal blitz, the scoreboard read, 'Ferguson 4 Ipswich 1'.

3 Before twice scoring for City in a stirring comeback, Thompson had already netted an own goal to put West Ham 2–0 ahead.

4 Jim Melrose.

5 Speedie scored a hat-trick of headers against Boro, which he managed again later in the season in a 5–0 win over Sheffield Wednesday.

6 First away hat-trick in thirty-three years.

7 Frank Leboeuf.

8 Macclesfield Town in the FA Cup and then Nottingham Forest a week later in the Premiership.

9 Mick Quinn in a famous 3–0 away win at Highbury in 1993.

10 Gary McSheffrey.

# Round 11

# Through the Ranks

1 Dennis Mortimer.
2 Andy Blair.
3 Gary McSheffrey.
4 Callum Davenport.
5 Chris Kirkland.
6 Kevin Thornton.
7 Gäel Bigirimana.
8 Christ the King.
9 Nathan Cameron.
10 Cyrus Christie and Callum Wilson.

1  43.
2  42.
3  David Icke.
4  Jim Blyth.
5  Les Sealey.
6  David Speedie took over and only let in 1 goal.
7  Gary Montgomery, who later went on to play cricket.
8  Stephen Hughes took over and kept a clean sheet.
9  Keiren Westwood.
10  Ryan Allsop, Jamie Jones and Lee Burge.

# Debuts

1 Perry Suckling.

2 Lloyd McGrath.

3 Greg Downs and Brian Borrows.

4 Marcus Hall.

5 Alex Evtushok.

6 Lee Carsley and Gary McSheffrey.

7 He vomited on the pitch!

8 Johnson scored twice against Bradford City – Quinn scored twice against Manchester City in 1992, while Keane scored twice against Derby in 1999.

9 Seven players made their debuts: Ryan Allsop, Réda Johnson, Jim O'Brien, Danny Swanson, Danny Pugh, Marcus Tudgay and Josh McQuoid.

10 Adam Armstrong, Ruben Lameiras, Romain Vincelot and Sam Ricketts.

# Round 14

# Bargain Basement

1 Stuart Pearce.
2 Steve Ogrizovic.
3 Brian Kilcline.
4 Peter Ndlovu.
5 Sean Flynn.
6 David Busst.
7 Dion Dublin.
8 George Boateng.
9 Michael Mifsud.
10 Kevin Malaga and William Edjenguélé.

1 Trevor Peake describing his central-defensive partner Brian Kilcline.
2 Mick Quinn after scoring twice in a 5–1 win against Liverpool in 1992.
3 Noel Whelan.
4 Ex-City Chairman Bryan Richardson talking about his manager Gordon Strachan.
5 Darren Huckerby.
6 After a brief City stay, which yielded 6 goals in 12 games, John Hartson made the claim shortly before leaving for Celtic!
7 Iain Dowie.
8 Aidy Boothroyd.
9 Steven Pressley.
10 Carl Baker.

# The League Cup

**1** 8–1.

**2** City came from 2–0 down to win the first leg 3–2, before bowing out 2–0 in the second leg at Upton Park.

**3** Steve Livingstone.

**4** Stuart Pearce scored the goal that sent Forest to Wembley.

**5** After 35 minutes City led 4–0, but after 53 minutes Forest had completed an unbelievable comeback to level things up at 4–4. City's Steve Livingstone hit the winner on 62 minutes.

**6** City memorably won 2–0 at Old Trafford!

**7** Michael Owen, then of Newcastle United, scored the winner in the extra period.

**8** Two leagues lower – City were in the Championship and Morecambe were in League Two.

**9** The caretaker boss was Richard Shaw.

**10** City lost 6–1 at the Emirates and loan striker Callum Ball hit the City goal.

1 Lloyd McGrath.
2 Houchen watched the 1986 Cup Final on TV at Newport & District Working Men's club in Middlesbrough.
3 Before each round Greaves kept on predicting City would be knocked out. As the team progressed further into the competition the joke and the chant grew.
4 The team went down to Bournemouth for general rest and relaxation, including golf, alcohol and tactics!
5 Dave Bennett had been a losing finalist for Manchester City in 1981 against Tottenham.
6 Welsh international Dave Phillips.
7 Houchen's goals were:

| | |
|:---|:---|
| Fourth round: | Man United away at Old Trafford |
| Sixth round: | Sheffield Wednesday (2 goals) away at Hillsborough |
| Semi-final: | Leeds United at Hillsborough |
| Final: | Tottenham Hotspur at Wembley. |

8 From a hospital bed after injuring his knee in the last game of the season against Southampton the week before.
9 The fountains in the town centre were dyed sky blue!
10 250,000.

# The Dreaded Drop

1   8 goals in total.
2   John Hartson.
3   Gary McAllister, then playing for Liverpool.
4   Villa Park.
5   'We'll be back.'
6   The diamond formation.
7   A red card in a 2–1 home defeat against Burnley.
8   Jutkiewicz scored 9 goals before he left, while his replacement Alex Nimely scored only once in the second half of the season.
9   Scored 3 times in a game.
10  Only 1 – away at Hull.

1  1969 was the year Armstrong walked on the moon,
   and the year Sky Blue Sam debuted for City!
2  They both worked in mines before becoming
   professional footballers.
3  Gerrard gave Thomas a lift to training when Thomas was
   loaned to Liverpool in January 2011.
4  Beckham famously scored from inside his own half against
   Wimbledon in 1995, and Baker did the same for City
   against Rotherham in 2014.
5  They both made their international debuts for England
   against Chile in 1998, and they shared the Golden Boot
   that same season.
6  Cody McDonald and Olly Murs were once striking partners
   for non-league Isthmian Division One North side
   Witham Town.
7  Both have two European Cup winners medals in their
   collections, Giggs played in the 1999 and 2008 finals while
   Oggy was an unused Liverpool substitute in the 1978 and
   1981 finals.
8  They each played top-flight football in four separate
   decades for Oggy, the 1970s, '80s, '90s and 2000s.
9  The nickname 'The Edge'!
10 Barton was once instrumental in an Arctic Monkeys
   tribute band around Clitheroe.

# The Bosses

1 Terry Butcher, Gordon Strachan, Roland Nilsson and Gary McAllister.
2 Terry Butcher in a Zenith Data tie against Aston Villa.
3 Bobby Gould, Mickey Adams and Steven Pressley.
4 In the League Cup Iain Dowie's men beat Man United 2–0 at Old Trafford and, in the same season in the FA Cup, they beat Mark Hughes' Blackburn 4–1 at Ewood Park.
5 Roland Nilsson in 2002 and Eric Black in 2004.
6 Steve Ogrizovic and Trevor Peake.
7 Chris Coleman.
8 Boothroyd's men peaked at fourth in the Championship before a post-Christmas slump.
9 Thorn was a chief scout.
10 Andy Thorn, Richard Shaw, Mark Robbins, Lee Carsley and Steven Pressley.

# Who am I?

1  All-time leading scorer Clarrie Bourton was a hat-trick specialist hitting 13 in total.

2  Bobby Gould played for and twice managed City.

3  George Curtis.

4  Ian Wallace successfully partnered Mick Ferguson and later became the first City player sold for £1 million.

5  Brian Borrows who played for Everton and Bolton and who sadly missed the FA Cup Final through injury.

6  Richard Shaw – the Frenchman was Eric Cantona who famously flew into the crowd at Selhurst Park moments after lashing out at Shaw and being sent off.

7  *Stern* John.

8  Gary McSheffrey first played in a 4–1 win at Villla Park in 1999 and has since gone on to play for Luton, Birmingham and Scunthorpe amongst others.

9  John Fleck, whose uncle Robert Fleck played for Norwich City, Chelsea and Scotland.

10  Steven Pressley played for City for one year in the mid-1990s. It was a mixed season for the young centre-back; while his physical presence was a positive, a glut of cards and penalties conceded was a minus. Pressley's line that 'things were far from ideal' was a massive understatement considering he put up with no home ground, transfer embargoes and a 10-point deduction!

# Spot Kicks

1. Jim Blyth.
2. Ian Painter hit the underside of the bar, the ball stayed out and City won 1–0.
3. The Simod Cup.
4. Brian Kilcline.
5. He hit it high over the crossbar in front of the East Stand as it was being redeveloped – rumours circulated that it was later found in a pub in Ball Hill!
6. Dion Dublin, David Burrows and rookie striker Simon Haworth.
7. Steve Ogrizovic who saved one kick.
8. City won 10–9 in a twenty-two-kick shoot-out. The first eighteen kicks were all converted before Murphy came into his own with two saves and the winning goal.
9. Goalkeeper Joe Murphy.
10. Leon Clarke, Callum Wilson, Carl Baker, Réda Johnson, Marcus Tudgay and Gary Madine.

# Big Mouth
# Strikes Again!

1  Jimmy Hill describing George Curtis.
2  After City won the Cup, Sillett was setting his sights high.
3  Atkinson quipped, 'If the *Titanic* had been painted Sky Blue it would never have sank'.
4  Strachan was talking about Darren Huckerby.
5  Richard Keys was firmly put in his place by a fuming Ron Atkinson after City lost a crucial game at Southampton in 1996. Atkinson firmly rejected Keys' ideas about the City players not having put enough into the game.
6  Craig Bellamy.
7  Peter Reid talking about how success at Sunderland changed his mindset. While at Highfield Road, Reid's Superman qualities seemed to be absent!
8  Mark Robbins in early 2013 – he left within weeks.
9  SISU's Joy Seppala.
10  Steven Pressley was talking about the difficulties of keeping cool during a 3–1 win at Rotherham which saw him sent to the stands after barely half an hour.

1  City beat Bayern Munich 2–1.
2  Bryan Richardson.
3  Four successive 0–0 draws.
4  Won the FA Cup with Wimbledon.
5  Engineering.
6  Was a policeman.
7  Training horses.
8  A hit record with Showaddywaddy.
9  Biking to Tile Hill and getting the train.
10  Twenty-six loans in two seasons.

# Would You Believe It?

1 Hunt's famous 'Donkey Kick' goal was outlawed by FIFA, who did not like the two-footed 'flip' from Willie Carr that put the ball into orbit.

2 The Talbot 'T' kit was banned as it pre-dated the days when all teams played with sponsors' logos emblazoned on their shirts.

3 Stocker had put £1,000 on City to win the FA Cup in 1987 at odds of 50–1.

4 Strachan took offence at some of the gestures a group of teenagers offered him from the back of a Warwickshire bus as he drove along. The City boss waited until he could nip in front of the bus and then parked up, before going on to give the youngsters a piece of his mind!

5 Kirkland's dad tells the story, 'He was 14 or 15 at the time and my family, friends and work colleagues put a bet of £100 at 100 to one' that Chris would play for England. In 2006, the bet paid dividends to the tune of almost £10,000.

6 Striker Leon Best sported a 'Zorro' mask as protection for a cheekbone fracture during the 2009 cup run. His superhero qualities came to the fore when he scored the fifth-round winner against Blackburn looking like a masked outlaw!

7 When the 10-year-old Bigirimana was sent shopping by his mum for milk at Asda, he took a detour to the Alan Higgs Centre across the road. Bigirimana had hopes of playing for a team, so he asked if he could play and was told to call back the next day, when his talent became clear to see.

8 Ken Delieu, Head of Football Operations at the time, caused a storm by sitting on the first-team bench against Hull in 2011, much to manager Andy Thorn's bemusement/anger/embarrassment.

9 In different circumstances, half-way through three successive seasons City lost leading goalscorers Lukas Jutkiewicz, David McGoldrick and Leon Clarke.

10 Mowbray was surprised to discover no scouting system was in place for new recruits!

# The Numbers Game

1  City have been champions three times: Division Three South, 1936; Division Three, 1964; Division Two, 1967.
2  Bourton scored a club record of 50 goals in one season, including seven hat-tricks.
3  Farmer converted twenty-two out of twenty-three spot kicks.
4  241 successive games.
5  £6.5 million.
6  City have not had a top-six finish in any division for forty-five years!
7  City registered no away victories in the league that season.
8  298 games.
9  1950s – keeper Reg Matthews.
   1980s – full-back Danny Thomas and striker Cyrille Regis.
   1990s – striker Dion Dublin.
10 34 miles from home!

# Absent Friends

1  Alan Brazil and Mick Quinn work for national radio station, TalkSport.
2  Greg Downs became a policeman after retiring from football.
3  Chris Waddle – who City once rejected!
4  Michael Gynn became a local postman.
5  Strong-arm stopper Brian Kilcline.
6  Terry Butcher.
7  Dion Dublin.
8  Claus Jørgensen now runs a successful floor cleaning and maintenance company based in Warwick.
9  After retiring from professional football, Leon McKenzie took up boxing and is now a super middleweight boxer.
10  Arjan de Zeeuw retired from playing in 2009 and took up a new career as a detective specialising in forensics.

# Premier League

1 After three straight wins, City were the first Premier League leaders.

2 Singing scouser and future Eurovision contestant Sonia provided the half-time cheer – although she was booed!

3 Ron Atkinson loved his sunglasses, whatever the weather.

4 Atkinson was 'moved upstairs' to become the Director of Football.

5 City took to the field at Ewood Park sporting lurid purple-and-yellow striped shirts with purple shorts and yellow socks.

6 Ball mistakenly thought Manchester City's 2–2 scoreline with Liverpool would secure their safety so he urged the team to keep possession rather than score a winning goal which would have sent Coventry down instead of Man City.

7 Strachan was 40 years old for his first start of the season and he played a blinder as City won 3–1.

8 Dublin and Owen each hit 18 Premiership goals to finish as joint top scorers.

9 Keane was sold for £13 million to Inter Milan in 2000.

10 Gary McAllister left on a free transfer to Liverpool, Noel Whelan was sold to Middlesborough and Steve Ogrizovic retired.

# Countdown

**10** Dave Phillips, Brian Kilcline, Trevor Peake, Greg Downs, Dave Bennett, Lloyd McGrath, Michael Gynn, Nick Pickering, Cyrille Regis and Keith Houchen.

**9** Gordon Strachan, Roland Nilsson, Gary McAllister, Eric Black, Peter Reid, Mickey Adams, Iain Dowie, Chris Coleman, Aidy Boothroyd, Andy Thorn, Mark Robbins, Steven Pressley, Tony Mowbray …

**8** Noel Cantwell, Gordon Milne, Dave Sexton, Bobby Gould, Don MacKay, John Sillett, Terry Butcher, Bobby Gould, Phil Neal, Ron Atkinson, Gordon Strachan.

**7** *Recognised left-backs:* Chris Hussey, Stephen O'Halloran, Martin Cranie, Blair Adams, Danny Pugh, Réda Johnson, Ryan Haynes, Chris Stokes …
*Filling in at left-back:* Jordan Clarke, Cyrus Christie, Richard Wood, Jordan Willis …

**6** Keiren Westwood, Michael Quirke, Joe Murphy, Chris Dunn, Lee Burge, Ryan Allsop, Jamie Jones, Reice Charles-Cook.

**5** Morocco: Mustapha Hadji, Youssef Chippo, Youssef Safri.
Ghana: Nii Lamptey.
Cameroon: Patrick Suffo.
Zimbabwe: Peter Ndlovu.

**4** Highfield Road (third round *v.* Bolton), Old Trafford (fourth round *v.* Man United), Victoria Ground (fifth round *v.* Stoke City) and Hillsborough (quarter-final *v.* Sheffield Wednesday and semi-final *v.* Leeds United)

**3** Robbie Keane £6 million in 1999, Craig Bellamy £6.5 million in 2000 and Lee Hughes £5 million in 2001.

**2** George Curtis and Mick Coop.

**1** Gordon Strachan refused to leave the field for 10 minutes. After an initial yellow card, Strachan was given his marching orders for comments made about the referee – Strachan maintains it was not him who made the disparaging remarks.

# What Happened Next?

1 City's Romanian striker Viorel Moldovan netted the
   rebound to score the match-winning goal in the FA Cup
   fifth-round tie against local rivals Aston Villa. The victory
   was City's first-ever win at Villa Park; it came at the twenty-
   seventh attempt, spanning sixty-two years. Moldovan did
   not achieve much in his spell at Highfield Road, but that
   1 goal secured his place in the affections of all Sky Blues' fans.

2 Noel Whelan moved into manager Gordon Strachan's
   house for six weeks to get back on the straight and narrow.

3 After McAllister's majestic strike, a young female fan ran
   onto the pitch topless and gave big Mo Konjic a kiss!

4 Young full-back Andy Whing thumped home a shot from
   the edge of the penalty area, to score the last ever goal at
   Highfield Road after 106 years (City beat Derby 6–2).

5 Despite being unbeaten in a moderate start, manager Andy
   Thorn was sacked.

6 Wilson ran speedily to the right-hand corner of the penalty
   area before leaving the defender for dead and firing home
   his first professional league goal. Only two years on, it's
   already the first of many.

7 Of the 27,306 crowd against Gillingham, only 11,085 made
   the next home match – 16,221 fans went somewhere else.

8 After tumbling over taking the ball, Burge inexplicably
   kicked out at Worcester player and was shown a straight
   red card. This started a disastrous afternoon that saw City
   humbled by non-leaguers once again.

**9** City lost the 3 games by a combined aggregate of 18–2 in what has been dubbed the 'worst week in their history'. The U21s suffered a 7–0 drubbing at Sheffield on the Monday before the first team were hammered 3–0 by Swindon live on TV that same evening. To finish the dismal week off, the Sky Blues youth team were thrashed 8–2 at Manchester City's purpose-built youth-team stadium.

**10** Rodger played the ball down the right flank to Lloyd McGrath whose cross was deflected off Gary Mabbutt's knee into the Tottenham net to win the 1987 FA Cup!

Also from The History Press

# *BACK OF THE NET!*

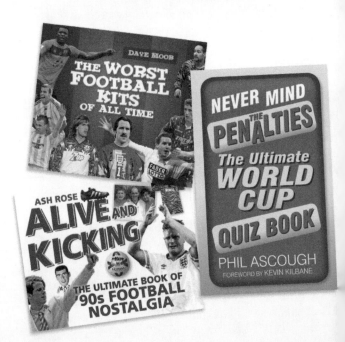

Also from The History Press

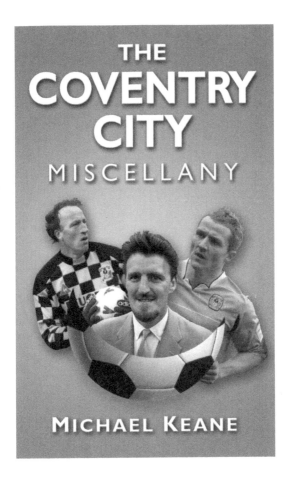

THE
COVENTRY
CITY
MISCELLANY

MICHAEL KEANE